Workbook

For

Bessel van der Kolk's

The Body Keeps The Score

Brain, Mind and Body in The Healing of Trauma

Genie Reads

Table of Contents

How To Use This Workbook

Hello there!

It is a great pleasure to see that you have taken an interest in the book "The Body Keeps The Score" by Bessel van der Kolk. This book by van der Kolk is groundbreaking and instrumental in shaping the way we view and treat trauma. Going beyond the medical norms in this day and age, we learn that trauma and its effective treatment can be deceptively simple. It isn't always necessary to rely on medication, and sometimes the most potent of treatments do not involve any drugs at all.

This workbook is meant to enhance and highlight the ideas and concepts mentioned, so that it makes it very much easier for you to take action and implement what you have learnt from the book into practical, daily usage. With the aid of this workbook, reviewing traumatic experiences and actually overcoming them becomes that much easier. Equipped with the knowledge and practical skillsets developed through the workbook's exercises, you will be better placed to address trauma wherever and whenever it happens. In order to learn quicker and with a lasting impact, it is vital that you answer all the questions presented in the workbook, and answer them sincerely. Only by digging deep and giving honest answers will you be able to flash light on what truly matters to you, and get the opportunities to effect lasting positive change in your daily life.

The workbook will also feature important summaries of each individual chapter, which will be integral in helping you answer the questions contained therein. As such, for the time constrained folk, you do not necessarily need to read the main book before answering the questions in this workbook. All the crucial points have been condensed and captured for your attention. For the folks whom have already read the book, the afore mentioned salient concepts will serve well as quick reminders and gentle nudges when you are doing the questions.

Whilst attempting the questions found in the workbook, please take your time to go through it carefully. This portion is an area where speedy reading can be set aside and replaced with thoughtful ruminations. The questions will encourage you to reflect and think, sometimes very deeply, before you jump in with any answers. It will be of great benefit to you if the answers supplied are colored with the honesty of thought and tinged with sincerity. After all, no one can be as interested in your welfare as your own self.

Done in this careful, constructive way, you will be able to harness the positive change created and see it reverberate throughout many aspects of your life. For some, the honest answers may create self criticism. Take heart, know that you are not alone, and that by just the mere act of acknowledgement of mistakes made in the past, that itself is a very important step forward.

You will want to come back to these questions again after your initial foray, say after a period of 4 to 8 weeks; there really is no set in stone time length, but it is highly recommended to have at least a space of 4 weeks between the first and second attempt at the questions. This second try is really to let you see the progress you have made, both in thoughts and actions, and also to think of different angles to the same questions with your new life experiences.

You can really repeat this process as many times as you find useful. The key is always honesty in the answers and an indefatigable spirit for self development and progress.

May you be well and be happy.

Introduction

We all experience trauma but in varying intensity – an abused person, an accident victim, or a survivor of war or disaster. Those who witness a horrifying or disastrous situation or by merely being around people who fell victim to such situations may be traumatized as well. For example, war survivors are more likely to suffer from post-traumatic stress disorder, and its lingering effects can scar the people around them.

Humans are known to be resilient, and in the face of trauma, we try to blot out the experience from our minds, live as normally as possible, and move on. However, the human brain will not allow us to forget the trauma easily. The slightest hint of danger, a sound, word, person, place, or event that reminds us of the experience could be sufficient to trigger an adverse reaction. Each recollection can become overwhelmingly painful and disturbing such that a traumatized person might feel out of control.

Until recently, even psychiatrists had very little knowledge about the science behind trauma. Thanks to modern scientific studies, three new branches of science emerged – all of which pertain to how the brain works. Neuroscience focuses on the brain and its impact on behavior and mental processes; developmental psychology deals with how toxic experiences affect the mind and the brain's development; and interpersonal neurobiology, which explains how our behavior affects biology, emotions, and mentality of the people around us.

Based on these new scientific fields, it has been ascertained that trauma creates changes in the brain, causing toxic behaviors such as anxiety, depression, rebellion, submissiveness, etc. These rob traumatized people of their self-esteem and prevent them from living everyday life.

The additional knowledge that resulted from years of research has led to discovering at least three opportunities to reverse or lessen the damage. One is by connecting with others. Another is through medication, and yet another is to go through experiences that cancel out the negative emotions brought about by trauma such as anger or helplessness. There is no single best way for a traumatized person to reverse the damage; sometimes, a person would need a combination of options.

The challenge for anyone who has gone through a traumatic experience is the restoration of their self-control. The purpose of the book is to help its readers face the horror of trauma and overcome its ill effects.

At the end of each chapter is a summary of lessons learned. Where appropriate, you will find questions on the issues relevant to the lessons, a suggested goal, a set of action steps, and a checklist to help you apply each chapter's insights. These sections do not attempt to resolve the trauma or replace professional help but to create awareness.

PART ONE:
THE REDISCOVERY OF TRAUMA

Ch 1: Lessons from Vietnam Veterans

Summary

Tom graduated valedictorian from high school. After his graduation, Tom enlisted in the Marine Corps to fulfill his father's expectation – to continue the family's tradition of serving in the military. Tom became a US Marine and was deployed to the Vietnam War as a platoon leader.

People sent to war are sufficiently trained, but they are aware that they need each other to survive the dangers of war. They support each other, help one another bear the loneliness of being away from their families, and form a special bond with each other. When comrades die at their enemies' hands, the survivors feel compelled to seek revenge for their fallen comrades. Tom was not different. He witnessed how a friend died in one of the enemies' attacks and decided to avenge his friend's death. Tom killed innocent people and raped a Vietnamese woman.

After being honorably discharged upon completion of his tour of duty, Tom pursued a college education and became a lawyer. He married his high school sweetheart and started his own family. Outwardly, it would seem Tom was living a normal, happy life. But he felt hollow. Tom is an influential lawyer and thrived while working on the cases he handled. However, when the case was over, he would lose his sense of purpose and become lost again.

Behind the normal life he projected, Tom came back from the war emotionally and psychologically wounded. Horrid nightmares haunted him, so Tom opted to stay up and drink until he passed out on the couch. He was given a prescription to lessen his nightmares' frequency and impact but never took any of it. Tom felt that by making the nightmares go away, he was disloyal to his friends who did not survive Vietnam.

Even long after he was discharged, Tom still dreaded the Fourth of July celebrations because the festivities triggered his memories of the Vietnam war – the sound and smell of the fireworks, the noisy crowd, etc. He preferred to flee his house and ride his Harley-Davidson to spare his family from his damaging behavior when he gets too upset because of the noise.

Tom's case is something that a lot of war survivors go through. Being there to experience the pain first-hand can be shattering, and having vivid memories of the war, overwhelming. They turn to drugs and alcohol to deaden the pain.

The sounds reminiscent of an ambush, the guilt of failing to save their comrades, and the shame of retaliating through atrocious acts continue to haunt survivors long after being discharged from military service. These toxic emotions aggravate the deep trauma of seeing their comrades die. War survivors cannot trust themselves to do it right by others, so they avoid intimate relationships.

After the war, veterans seem to limit their circle of meaningful relationships to fellow veterans. They cannot trust people who have not been to war – even their families, friends, or co-workers. War veterans are animated when they talk about their war experiences but cringe when asked to talk about other life experiences.

War survivors suffer from flashbacks. A slight reminder of what it was like at war – an image, a sound, a smell, a feeling – can trigger a sense of panic. There is no telling what or when a flashback will occur or stop.

Nightmares and flashbacks are not exclusive to war veterans; other trauma victims have them, too. These victims are battling their own war – for some, their war happens inside their homes as they fall victim to either domestic violence or rape or both. The challenge of healing is much more complex when the victims are children.

Trauma victims tend to get stuck in their past and lose their ability to imagine. The failure to imagine means no dreams to pursue, no motivation for a better life, and no chance of enriching relationships with people who matter to them.

Traumatized people perceive things differently from other people. For example, a man accidentally bumps into a woman in a crowded place. Some women will see it as just an accident, but a sexually abused woman might look at that incident as a threat.

Three decades of research has led to a better understanding of trauma. A traumatic experience leaves an indelible mark on our body, brain, and mind, affecting our core being.

Trauma alters our ability to think. It causes severe damage that can only be reversed when the body acknowledges that the danger is no longer there. Only then can a traumatized person live in the present.

Lessons

1. The effect of trauma on people can be deep-seated; it haunts the victim even long after the traumatic incident.

2. The manifestations of trauma on returning soldiers and war veterans may be experienced by others who suffer from a different kind of trauma, e.g., physical abuse.

3. Wealth, accolades, and accomplishments cannot obliterate trauma.

Issues Surrounding the Subject Matter

1. What measures or programs have been put in place to counter the effects of trauma?

2. Have you had a traumatic experience? If you have not, has someone close to you been in a trauma? What is it about?

Goals

1. How do you intend to recover from your trauma? Or how do you intend to help your friend recover from the trauma?

Action Steps

1. Describe the traumatic incident you or someone close to you experienced. Label your feelings when you were in that situation.

2. Document your thoughts and your feelings as you recall your traumatic experience.

Checklist

1. Use a journal to record the information requested above.

2. Be candid with your description. It does not matter if you write the events in the correct sequence or not.

3. The description need not be in narrative form. You might want to illustrate it or do a poem. Use whatever format you are comfortable with.

Ch 2: Revolutions in Understanding Mind and Brain

Summary

Patients in a research ward at Massachusetts Mental Health Center (MMHC) exhibited seemingly baseless outbursts, panicked withdrawal, muddled speech, complex logic, open conversations, and lack of physical coordination.

Elvin Semrad, a well-loved and influential psychiatrist, taught that healing could only occur when a patient acknowledges the reality of what they know and feel. He said that the therapists' role is to help the patients "acknowledge, experience, and bear" that reality.

However, medical professionals took on a different approach that focused more on discovering drugs to correct mental "disorders." The administration of antipsychotic drugs succeeded in significantly reducing the number of patients residing in mental hospitals in America.

The field of neuroscience did several experiments to answer questions about traumatic stress. One such experiment placed dogs in locked cages where they were repeatedly subjected to electric shock. The study showed that the traumatized dogs did not leave the cage even when given a chance. They had to be repeatedly pulled out from the cage to physically experience and learn to get out from a harmful environment. However, further studies on animals revealed that traumatized animals return home, whether the home is safe or not.

The results of these experiments point to several similarities with traumatized people. Despite the fear and grief they experienced in combat, Vietnam war veterans seem to come alive when recalling their helicopter crashes and dying comrades' experiences. We also hear of sexually or physically abused women who seek abusive relationships later in life.

Freud calls this tendency "the compulsion to repeat." Traumatized people instinctively re-create the toxic experiences, hoping to master a painful situation and resolve it for good. However, repeating the experience merely aggravates the pain and leads to self-loathing.

An earlier study explained how fear- or pain-inducing experiences excite some people and make them crave it. For instance, extreme sports may be dreadful at first but can become an exhilarating and pleasurable experience. The shift from dread to excitement means that our body has reached a new chemical balance. We begin to seek that feeling, and the failure to find it leads to withdrawal. Eventually, we become more focused on the agony of withdrawal, which explains why some people intentionally hurt themselves or get drawn to people who hurt them.

Based on neuroscientific studies, our brain produces a morphine-like substance, known as endorphin, when we are under stress. This finding is one reason why traumatized people want to re-live the stress – the level of endorphins released blocks the pain of the experience. Another finding says that we become more aggressive as the level of serotonin in our brain decreases.

The advancements in neuroscience encouraged pharmaceutical companies to develop new products to address traumatic stress and its symptoms. Fluoxetine, better known by its brand name Prozac, is one of the most efficacious drugs developed. However, based on a study, Prozac has no positive effect on people with PTSD.

Psychiatry benefitted from pharmacology's headway. Apart from offering an alternative to talk therapy, the success of Prozac and similar medications created a domino effect: the new products brought more income and profit to pharmaceutical companies, enabling these companies to fund grants for further studies. The grants provided for more modern and sophisticated laboratories and instruments. Although these drugs enabled the patients to function day-to-day, core issues are not adequately addressed, so that patients are unable to regain complete control of their lives. Funding for the research of non-drug treatments of mental health problems is scarce, and those who explore such options are dismissed as "alternative. "

Ironically, despite the continued increase in antidepressants, the number of people admitted for depression has likewise increased. Antipsychotic drugs also put children who take them at risk for diabetes and obesity.

The studies done so far failed to consider four fundamental truths:

- Healthy relationships breed healthy well-being.
- Communication allows us to change ourselves, influence others, and share a common purpose with them.
- We can control how our body and brain function.
- We can help create a safe environment for both children and adults.

When we recognize and apply these truths, we can help people heal from trauma and empower them to regain their self-esteem.

Lessons

1. Healing from trauma can only take place when the victim learns to accept the reality.

2. People in trauma feel compelled to "repeat" the experience, hoping to be in control the next time it happens.

3. The effectiveness of antipsychotic drugs has not reduced the number of depression cases in the United States.

4. The search for healing trauma interventions must consider the need for healthy relationships, honest communication, body- and brain-control, and a safe environment.

Issues Surrounding the Subject Matter

1. What makes it difficult for a trauma victim to accept reality?

2. What problems does a "compulsion to repeat" the traumatic experience bring to the trauma victim?

3. Why is the number of depression cases rising despite the discovery of efficacious antipsychotic drugs?

Goals

1. What should you do to make it easier to accept reality?

2. What can you do to alleviate the ill-effects of the trauma?

Action Steps

1. Create a 3-column table on one sheet of your journal. Label it "Addressing Trauma."
    a. In the first column, write down the action (s) you have taken to relieve yourself from the trauma's pain.
    b. On the second column, indicate the effect of the action you took.
    c. On the third column, indicate the truth that corresponds to the effect.

2. On another sheet in your journal, create a 2-column table. Label the table, "My Reality."
    a. In the first column, write down the challenges that prevent you from facing your reality.
    b. On the second column, indicate which of the four truths is (are) related to each challenge.

3. Compare the two tables you created. Identify which truth you need to work on and briefly describe what you intend to do about it.

Checklist

1. Prepare your journal.

2. Be as detailed as possible. For example, in action step 2, column 1: instead of writing, "unexpected," you may

write, "I have always been a careful driver and I can't believe I hit an old lady."

3. Refer to the four truths mentioned in this chapter.

Ch 3: Looking into the Brain: The Neuroscience Revolution

Summary

A study was made on what goes on in the brains of traumatized people when flashbacks occur. In the study, eight participants listened to a voice recording of a script based on their respective traumatic experiences. The study confirmed that deep emotions activate the brain's limbic system, which deals with emotions and memory. Specifically, it stimulates the amygdala, which warns us of impending danger and prepares us for our body's fight/flight response.

The study further revealed the following:

- The Broca's area, responsible for producing speech, fails to function correctly when a flashback is triggered, like in stroke patients. When the Broca's area does not function, a traumatized person may refuse to speak, scream, or zone out. When they regain their ability to speak, trauma patients talk about their tragic experiences but cannot relate their stories coherently.

- Trauma activates Brodmann's area 19, which is responsible for the visual association. This area of the brain records images as they enter the brain but hearing the voice recording set off the area as if the trauma is happening.

- Flashbacks trigger the brain's right side, which performs emotional, intuitive, visual, tactile functions. The left brain disengages, and the patient fails to recognize what they are going through is just a re-creation of an experience; instead, the patient feels the same intense emotions as if the incident is taking place in the present.

A threatening situation causes our stress hormones to spike; one of these hormones is adrenaline. As the adrenaline increases during a flashback, so does a traumatized person's heart rate and blood pressure. It also takes longer for a traumatized person's level of stress hormones to return to normal, which makes them prone to irritability, lack of attention, long-term health issues, memory problems, and sleep disorders.

Some people respond to threat by simply ignoring them and acting as if nothing has happened. This reaction can lead to an illness. Others turn to alcohol, drugs, or medication to reduce or wipe out the unpleasant feelings, but the relief they offer is only temporary.

Psychotherapy suggests talking as a way of addressing the ill feelings brought about by trauma. However, the effects of trauma itself prevent productive talk from happening because the rational brain is powerless to coax the reality of the emotional brain's experience.

Lessons

1. Our brain warns us of impending threats and influences our reaction to them.

2. In the face of danger, we respond in three ways: fight, flight, or freeze.

3. We experience intense emotions during a flashback because it deactivates the left side of our brain. The intensity during flashback may be as strong as the experience itself.

4. One of the interventions for dealing with trauma is talk therapy. It may be effective if the emotional brain does not overpower the rational brain.

Issues Surrounding the Subject Matter

1. What problems does talk therapy present to a trauma patient?

Goals

1. What should you do to help a trauma patient talk about their experience?

Action Steps

1. Encourage and join them in physical activities like running, walking, or swimming to burn off their brain's stress chemicals. These activities encourage better sleep so they can relax.

2. Try to get them to socialize slowly, starting with a small intimate group with whom they can feel safe. Find a way to include a funny or amusing story during this gathering to get them to smile or laugh, which is a good stress-reliever.

3. When they are ready to talk about the experience, listen to them without interruption. Do not mind the trauma victim if they get upset as they tell their story. Remain calm and continue to listen.

Checklist

1. Never force the victim to talk about their experience but assure them that you are there to listen if they are ready to talk about it.

2. Do not assume you know how the person feels or what is going on in their minds because you don't

3. Avoid using cliches' like "look at the brighter side" or "everything will be ok."

4. Do not insist on getting professional help. Each trauma victim responds differently to the same experience.

PART TWO: THIS IS YOUR BRAIN ON TRAUMA

Ch 4: Running for Your Life: The Anatomy of Survival

Summary

People with trauma cannot make sense of what they saw or experienced and get stuck with the negative emotions and thoughts that come with it. These people fail to incorporate new experiences into their lives.

A person who survives trauma loses spontaneity because their energy becomes too focused on controlling their turmoil. The attempt to control the internal chaos becomes too stressful, leading to a wide variety of physical symptoms. This explains the importance of involving the body, mind, and brain to fight trauma and its ill effects.

Our brain is responsible for safeguarding our survival, regardless of the situation we are in, and it can only happen through five essential functions:

- Generation of internal signals to identify our body's needs

- Creation of maps to lead us where to get our needs

- Generation of energy and action to get us what we need

- Alerting us of threats and opportunities as we get our needs

- Alteration of our actions according to what the current situation requires

Each brain structure plays a vital role in fulfilling these functions.

The reptilian brain controls our body's vital functions, including body temperature, breathing, and heart rate. It is responsible for what infants can do – touching, sleeping, crying, eating, urination, and defecation. Because these activities seem to be essential, their significance in trauma treatment is often ignored. But when any of these activities hit a snag, e.g., disrupted sleep, a sense of panic when touched, or feeling hunger pangs more than expected, we lose our internal balance. We may either cause trauma or prevent us from recovering from a traumatic experience.

The limbic system is the seat of our emotions and influences our behavior. It warns us against threats and helps us identify what we need to survive. This part of the brain includes the amygdala, which evaluates if incoming information is relevant to our survival. The amygdala works with the hypothalamus to enable us to respond to danger.

The part of the brain that takes care of our learning abilities is the neocortex. It enables us to develop abstract thinking, consciousness, imagination, and language.

The frontal lobes found in the neocortex allow us to process large volumes of information and be creative, plan, generate and make choices. The frontal lobes are responsible for empathy, which is crucial for nurturing relationships with others. The amygdala prepares us for a fight/flight/freeze response when the brain spots potential danger, but the frontal lobes allow us to evaluate if the danger is real.

Stress management requires a balance between the amygdala and the frontal lobes, specifically the medial prefrontal cortex (MPFC). There are two options for managing emotions:

- The top-down approach requires bolstering the frontal lobes' capacity to monitor bodily sensations, which can be done through mindfulness meditation and yoga.

- The bottom-up approach calls for a fine-tuning of the autonomic nervous system (ANS); touch, movement, and breathing can help with recalibration.

We experience our "normal self" when there is a balance between our emotional and rational brains. However, in the face of a threat or danger, they function independently. How we react will depend on which of the two is more dominant. Psychologists encourage the use of insight and understanding to manage behavior. But when the emotional brain persists in sending warning signals, insight and understanding will not quash the alarm.

The tug-of-war between our emotional and rational brains leads to physical and psychological distress.

The essence of trauma is dissociation – a process where the traumatic experience falls apart and the related emotions, thoughts, and sensations become harder to control.

A traumatic experience will end at some point, but flashbacks and the tendency to re-live the experience do not. Flashbacks can happen any time, and no one can tell when they will end. The more we replay the fragmented elements of the trauma in our minds, the deeper they get etched in our memory.

Trauma survivors get stuck in the past and find it challenging to live in the present. They react to situations differently – sometimes irrationally, alienating them from others. Shame becomes the foremost emotion, and these people become too preoccupied with hiding the truth.

The amygdala defines our experience's emotional intensity, but its context and meaning are defined by the brain system that houses the dorsolateral prefrontal cortex (DLFPC) and the hippocampus.

The DLFPC links our present experience to our past and predicts its potential impact on our future. For trauma survivors who realize that the experience will end sometime, the pain becomes more bearable. On the other hand, the person may feel excruciating pain and think of the experience as endless.

Recovery from trauma can only happen when the amygdala, the MPFC, and the DLFPC are activated. Therapy will be futile if the trauma survivor remains stuck in their past.

The thalamus is the seat of learning, concentration, and attention; trauma may impair all these functions. The thalamus works as a filter to separate relevant sensory information from those we can let go of. People suffering from PTSD lack this filter and are constantly overwhelmed by sensory information.

Depersonalization is another way of responding to trauma. A traumatized person dissociates from the experience and blanks out. Almost every part of their brain is deactivated, explaining the numb reaction. Conventional talk therapy does not work for such cases, making it more challenging to treat the trauma patient.

Treatment approaches that dwell on the past are not enough to heal a trauma patient. What is more important is to help them live productively and securely in the present.

Lessons

1. The stress brought on by trauma is too intense, so that a trauma victim suffers from stress-related illnesses, such as migraines.

2. Our brain needs to fulfill five functions to ensure our survival, each performed by a specific brain system.

3. The reptilian brain's importance in dealing with trauma is sometimes diminished because its functions are deemed fundamental. Yet, a problem with any of these may either add to the trauma or prevent recovery from trauma.

Issues Surrounding the Subject Matter

1. What are the disadvantages when you do things subconsciously because it has become a habit?

2. What are the potential problems if you are not aware of your habits?

3. Do you have a deeply-rooted habit that you find hard to change? What habit is this?

4. Think about the times where your reaction to certain events or matters was instantaneous or automatic, like polishing off that packet of potato chips before realizing you had really meant to just eat half. How did that make you feel deep down?

Goals

1. How can you help a trauma victim manage their stress?

Action Steps

You may add the following action steps to those listed in Chapter 3:

1. Find out what triggers the flashbacks or nightmares and try to avoid them. For example, if one of the triggers is the smell of a cigarette, avoid smoking near the trauma victim. If the smell of cigarettes cannot be avoided, ask the trauma victim to look around them and have them describe to you what they see. This practice will let them know that they are in the present.

2. Discover what makes the trauma victim feel safe. Strive to create that space for the victim. For example, you may create a playlist of piano music that the trauma

victim can play before sleeping. It could also mean allowing them to sleep with the lights on or have someone sleep with them in the same room if the trauma victim is comfortable with it.

3. Encourage a trauma victim to participate in decision-making to make them feel they still have control over some parts of their lives. If the trauma victim is a child, you may ask them to decide on simple things such as choose how to spend the weekend or what to have for dinner.

Checklist

1. Learn the signs that the trauma victim is "triggered," so you can help and prevent any adverse reaction.

2. Spend as much time as possible with the trauma victim without intruding on their privacy.

3. Be ready to feel tired and upset as you help the trauma victim. Feeling that way is normal; do not be guilty about those emotions. They do not mean you care less for the trauma victim.

Ch 5: Body-Brain Connections

Summary

According to Charles Darwin, humans are like animals in communicating emotions through their bodies. The interplay of facial expressions, postures, and tone of voice expresses hints at how a person feels and what goes on in their minds. Darwin further notes that a person in survival mode is too absorbed in waging war against an unseen enemy, rendering them incapable of caring, loving, and nurturing.

Intense negative emotions affect both the heart and the gut. Emotions that remain in our heads are controllable, but when we start feeling it on our guts, we will do everything to make them go away. Sometimes, the coping mechanisms we adopt do more harm than good, e.g., inflicting physical harm on self to distract from the emotional pain.

The autonomous nervous system (ANS) has two branches: the sympathetic nervous system (SNS) and parasympathetic nervous system (PNS). The SNS works with the emotions and triggers the release of adrenaline, increasing the blood pressure and speeding up the heart rate. It is also responsible for arousal and fight/flight response. The PNS counters the SNS's effect, slowing down the heart rate as it triggers acetylcholine release. We need to have a balance of SNS and PNS.

The Polyvagal Theory focuses on the relationship between our bodies' intuitive experiences and other peoples' faces and voices. Based on the theory, seeing a kind face or hearing a gentle voice can soothe and reassure us. It explains why focused attention given to a person helps them shift from a fearful to a secure state. People quickly sense slight emotional shifts in others by observing subtle body language. When other people send positive signals, it becomes easy for us to feel safe and supported.

We have always been told to recognize and celebrate our uniqueness. However, our brains are designed to function within society; we spend much energy connecting with others even when alone, e.g., preparing a presentation for a meeting.

Relationships that offer safety are essential to mental health and meaningful life. Social support is the most potent safeguard against stress and trauma. It is not about being around others, but about reciprocity, being seen and listened to.

Trauma victims seek solace in groups that share their backgrounds or experiences. However, when the group does not appreciate individuality and dismisses others' views as irrelevant, isolation intensifies.

When we are threatened, our impulse is to turn to the first level of safety, known as social engagement. We seek help and comfort from the people around us. The ventral vagal complex (VVC) is active at this level; it sends signals that make us feel calm, centered, and relaxed. It also helps us send distress signals if we sense any threat to our safety.

If the danger is immediate or we do not see anyone coming to our aid, the limbic system sets off, so we go to the second level: fight or flight. Danger deactivates our VVC, intensifies our sensitivity to threat signals, and spurs us into action.

If the fight-or-flight response fails, the dorsal vagal complex (DVC) is activated. It cuts our body's metabolism, decreases our heart rate, and our gut stops working. We save ourselves by going into a state of freeze or collapse.

Many traumatized folks have defensive system that are too strong such that they fail to enjoy life's pleasures, become numb to new experiences, or become too vigilant in looking for danger signals. Many people find safety in trivial conversations and overreact to physical contact, but we can enjoy genuine affection when we experience immobilization without fear.

Instead of focusing on the mind's cognitive capacities, it would be worthwhile to apply new approaches that focus on the emotional engagement system to break down a trauma victim's defensive barriers. Treatment strategies that combine the activation of social engagement with the relaxation of the body's physical tensions have been proven to work well.

Lessons

1. We can communicate our thoughts and feelings through our body language, facial expression, and voice tone. We can use them to send warning signals as well.

2. There are three response levels to a threat: social engagement, fight-or-flight, and freeze or collapse.

3. Not all strategies for coping with trauma are helpful.

4. Traumatized people tend to build high walls of defense and become hypervigilant to threats.

Issues surrounding the subject matter

1. What are the disadvantages of each level of safety or response to threat?

2. Why do trauma victims tend to adopt harmful coping mechanisms?

Goals

1. What can you do to break down your or a trauma victim's defensive walls?

Action Steps

1. Develop a keen sense of self-awareness.

2. Accept and recognize that you are using a form of defense mechanism.

3. Describe the effect of having that kind of defense—mention both the upside and downside.

Checklist

1. A defense mechanism can come in the form of denial, repression, projection or displacement, behaving differently from what you truly feel, rationalization, childish behavior, or avoidance.

2. There are various ways to develop self-awareness. Some of these are identified below. Choose one or two that suits you:

   a. Do a full-body scan and observe how you feel as you touch each part of your body.

   b. Do breathing exercises and observe how it affects your body and mind.

   c. Observe your actions, e.g., how long do you take a bath? Do you eat slowly? How patient are you about waiting?

Ch 6: Losing Your Body, Losing Yourself

Summary

Research shows that continued exposure to emotional abuse and neglect is as shattering as being a victim of physical and sexual molestation.

Our instinctive response to distress is to reach out to people we trust and like or engage in feel-good physical activities like biking. But in their absence, we experiment with other things that provide relief. Sometimes, our alternatives are equally dangerous.

People who suffer from trauma or neglect experience severe disconnection from the body; they tend to lose sensory perceptions.

Research revealed that when our idling brain, known as the default state network (DSN), is activated, we heighten our self-awareness. The DSN works together with the other self-sensing areas to bring us consciousness.

On the other hand, people with chronic PTSD have most of these self-sensing areas turned off. As they shut off the disturbing sensations, traumatized people also stifled their faculty to feel fully alive. The deactivation of these areas damages their inner reality. They lose their sense of purpose and the ability to decide wisely because they lose sight of who they are.

Antonio Damasio, the author of The Feeling of What Happens, says that people sometimes use the mind to put a screen over facts. The screen hides from the mind from getting clarity about the inner states of the body. Although this screen allows us to attend to severe external problems, it stops us from being in touch with our "self."

Our brain's subcortical regions control our breathing, digestion, heartbeat, hormone secretion, and immune system. But the presence of threat – perceived or actual - can overpower these systems, causing a broad range of physical problems. Our conscious self is crucial for maintaining our inner equilibrium.

Agency refers to the feeling of being in control of our life. It begins with interoception: our receptiveness to our subtle body-based feelings. As we increase the level of receptiveness, the more we can be in control of our lives.

Our gut feelings tell us what is safe or threatening and help us assess what is happening around us. However, traumatized people do not feel safe and choose to ignore internal warning signals. The more we disregard our sensory signals, the more we allow our trauma to own us. We also fail to distinguish what is genuinely safe or dangerous.

Many people with trauma suffer from alexithymia or the inability to label their feelings, which occurs because they do not know their physical sensations. Alexithymia patients are not aware of their needs, so they fail to take care of themselves. They also catalog their emotions as physical problems. Their intense negative emotions usually manifest as physical discomfort or illness. They react to stress either through anger or by zoning out.

The first step to trauma recovery is to be in touch with our body sensations and what they mean. Developing physical self-awareness can be distressing and may lead to flashbacks. Medications are often prescribed, but all they do is deaden the disturbing feeling but not resolve the problem.

People naturally calm down when they latch onto another person. This can pose a problem for sexually and physically abused women, and they must be helped to tolerate being touched gradually. They need to reconnect with themselves to develop genuine relationships. The faster one reconnects with self and others, the faster these victims can recover from the trauma.

Lessons

1. We are inclined to seek a person we trust or engage in physical activity when we are in distress.

2. People with PTSD lose their sense of identity and purpose.

3. Suffering from trauma causes us to lose our sense of self. However, we can avoid this loss if we are highly receptive to our physical sensations.

4. Unless we are in touch with our body sensations, we cannot progress towards recovery.

Issues surrounding the subject matter

1. What problems does a person with trauma face when they lose their sense of purpose?

2. What potential problems are there if our go-to coping mechanism for distress, e.g., a trusted person, is not available?

Goals

1. How do you regain your sense of purpose?

Action Steps

1. Write down your goal in your journal. Is this a new goal or something you lost when you had your trauma?

2. If it is a new goal, indicate why you decided to pursue a new goal.

3. List down the steps you need to do to pursue your goal.

4. Write down the names of persons you need or want to help you pursue your goal – it may be a business partner or just somebody to be there to help you.

Checklist

1. Creating a sense of purpose is not always about making money. It can be about making yourself useful to society, or it can be both. Keep your goal close to your interests. Pursue what you love to do.

2. Be sure to get the help of people with a positive attitude and support your goals.

3. Strive to meet new people who can help you achieve your purpose.

PART THREE:
THE MINDS OF CHILDREN

Ch 7: Getting on the Same Wavelength: Attachment and Attunement

Summary

A test was conducted to discover how children's reality affects their life views. Children who did not experience or witness abuse within their family projected a sense of security with their family. They felt the love of their parents, motivating them to learn and enjoy school. These children experienced and recognized bad situations but thought of ways to get out of them. The responses of children abused by their families were startling. They were shown images that depict everyday life, but all they saw was danger.

We learn about self-care from the way our caregivers cared for us as we were growing up. Children are hypersensitive to body language, facial expressions, and tone of voice and are wired to be attached to an adult who is most responsive to them.

However, not all attachments are secure. There must be emotional attunement between the child and the caregiver to create a haven for the child, and the attunement begins at infancy when the mother holds her baby. The baby senses it when the mother fails to meet the infant's needs and impulses and becomes vulnerable.

A secure attachment allows children to acquire a sense of agency, know when they can control a situation and seek help, and identify what makes them feel good and what makes them feel bad. They are also attuned to other people's feelings.

The combination of secure attachment and the encouragement to develop capabilities creates an internal locus of control for the child. This locus of control enables children to cope with different situations throughout their life. But abuse and neglect can topple a child's secure base. The need for attachment does not wane, and the moment a child feels a lack of connection, they will do anything to seek attention.

Children naturally attach themselves to their parents or caregivers, and they develop a coping mechanism to ensure that one of their needs is met. Three other attachment patterns emerged from research conducted to discover a baby's reaction to a temporary separation from the mother.

In the avoidant attachment, the babies did not cry when their mother left and ignored her when she came back. But the infants' heart rates increased, showing that they were stressed. Most mothers of avoidant infants are not fond of touching or cooing to their babies.

In the anxious or ambivalent attachment, the babies ensured that somebody paid attention to them by screaming, crying, or clinging. They were upset when their mother left, but the mother's return was not enough to appease the babies.

The third pattern is the disorganized attachment, where the caregivers themselves are the source of the children's distress. Children in this pattern do not know how to connect with their caregivers: they need their mothers to survive, but their mothers also terrify them. Parental abuse, parents suffering from trauma themselves, or the caregivers' insensitivity to the infants' cues may lead to this attachment pattern.

The attachment pattern a child develops in infancy is the same pattern that they are most likely to adopt when they grow older and determine how they cope with life's challenges. Securely attached infants communicate their frustrations, goals, fears, and interests. Those who grew up with disorganized attachment anticipate rejection, dissociate, and remain in a state of hyperarousal.

As adults, we can do something to restore equilibrium by exploring options to create healthy relationships.

<u>Lessons</u>

1. Children with loving and stable parents are secure, confident, and capable of giving love. Those who belong to dysfunctional parents are angry, anxious, afraid, and see danger in almost every event.

2. There are four types of attachment between a parent/caregiver and child: secure, avoidant, ambivalent, and disorganized.

3. A well-loved child's safety bubble may burst if the child is subjected to neglect or abuse.

<u>Issues surrounding the subject matter</u>

1. What problems does each attachment type present to the child and later, as an adult?

<u>Goals</u>

1. What must be done to ensure that children are securely attached growing up?

<u>Action Steps</u>

1. Describe your child. Write down the description. How would you classify your child's attachment?

2. List qualities about your child you adore.

3. List your child's qualities that are not so adorable.

4. Identify potential risks to your child's safety and emotional security.

5. If applicable, list qualities that your child adopted to adulthood.

6. Describe the actions you will take to protect your child.

Checklist

1. Refer to the description of the four types of attachment found in this chapter.

2. "Your child" refers to any child you would like to consider for this exercise. It could be your child, a sibling, a niece or nephew, or a friend's child. You may also decide to describe yourself as a child based on what you can recall.

3. If you choose to describe yourself as a child, change item 4 to actual risks; item 6 to actions you think should have taken to protect you from the risks.

Ch 8: Trapped in Relationships: The Cost of Abuse and Neglect

Summary

Our first caregivers influence our perception of reality and how we connect with them. They feed our brain with information that forms our inner maps. Our experiences as we grow older may alter these maps. For instance, experiencing true love may transform a broken child into an adult who is willing to trust and appreciate intimacy.

Unfortunately, being abused can also transform a pleasant childhood map into something ugly. We need to rewire our central nervous system, and the first step is to recognize irrational thoughts and behaviors.

Usually, the rational brain dominates the emotional brain, except when our fears control us. When we feel furious, rejected, or trapped, we become helpless and retrieve the old maps we have preprogrammed. We need to observe and bear our inner turmoil to acknowledge the emotions that keep our maps irreversible.

Children rely on their families for survival. When a family member physically or sexually abuses them, they have no one to ask for help. They cope by blocking off the experience from their minds and pretend that it never happened to them.

Children are wired to be loyal to their family or caregivers. However, loyalty to an abusive family translates into despair, helplessness, and loneliness. Unexpressed anger leads to self-loathing and self-destruction.

One way to counter these damaging effects is to differentiate what is real from imagined and learn to know who you can trust.

Lessons

1. A child's earliest caregiver, usually the mother, significantly influences the child's reality.

2. Inner maps that began to form in infancy may be revised by the child as they grow older, based on their experiences.

3. Children are dependent on their families for survival. They are not capable of leaving their family even if they have a toxic relationship.

4. Children are loyal to their families; they will stick it out and cover-up for their family's dysfunctionality despite the abuses.

Issues surrounding the subject matter

1. What problems can a child experience when they remain loyal to their abusive family? How will it impact the child when they turn into an adolescent? An adult?

Goals

1. What can you do to help a child from a dysfunctional family grow into a productive, balanced adult?

Action Steps

1. Encourage the child to talk about their feelings. Do not minimize the value of these emotions.

2. Find out what the child loves to do and seek opportunities for the child to enjoy it. For example, if the child loves playing with other kids, organize a playgroup for them.

3. When and where possible, give the child decision-making roles to feel important, e.g., what activity to do, what to eat, what game to play, etc.

Checklist

1. Listen attentively.

2. If the child does not want to talk about their feelings, have them express them in a different way, e.g., drawing

3. If the child chooses to cry, let them cry without stopping them. It might be their way of releasing all the pent-up emotions.

Ch 9: What's Love Got to Do with It?

Summary

Psychiatry attempts to have a clear-cut definition of mental illnesses, but the brain, mind, and human attachment systems are too complex for such precision. A psychiatric diagnosis determines treatment, which may end up badly if not done correctly. It also attaches a lifetime label to the patient, influencing how they define themselves.

A study was done to establish if borderline personality disorder (BPD) and childhood trauma are correlated. It uncovered that 81% of a hospital's patients diagnosed with BPD had histories of child abuse and neglect.

Children who suffer from such abuse and neglect experience intense, honest emotions, which they feel compelled to deny because acknowledging them would harm them. Disowning the experience leads to distrust of self and others, restrained curiosity, and the inclination to find the situation unreal.

Victims of childhood physical and sexual abuse are more prone to self-cutting and suicide attempts, probably as a means of escape or an attempt to feel a sense of self-control. An abused child with a recollection of feeling safe with someone once before can refresh that affection. Without that recall, the brain receptors responding to human kindness may not develop.

The Adverse Childhood Experience (ACE) study disclosed that childhood and adolescent trauma are more widespread than expected. Based on the same study, childhood sexual abuse may lead to alcoholism, drugs, morbid obesity, multiple sexual partners, and unintended pregnancies. These problems become adaptive tools helping the victims prevent a recurrence of the abuse.

Lessons

1. Children subjected to child abuse and neglect are more likely to suffer from a borderline personality disorder (BPD).

2. Abused and neglected children choose to deny the experience because they fear retaliation, which will hurt them more.

3. Based on a study, the problem of childhood and adolescent trauma is more extensive than it seems. It leads to other problems such as sexual promiscuity, obesity, drugs, among others.

4. An abused child who never felt loved may harbor bitterness because they never knew what love feels like.

Issues surrounding the subject matter

1. Why are child and adolescent trauma widespread?

Goals

1. What can you do to help children recover from trauma?

Action Steps

1. Enumerate the activities you are prepared to undertake to help children recover from trauma.

2. Explain briefly how each activity can achieve the goal.

Checklist

1. Remember to understand the background of the traumatized child. A child who has been physically or sexually abused may react negatively to touch, which is supposed to have a healing effect on other children.

2. Watch your body language, facial expression, and tone of voice when dealing with abused children.

3. Encourage children to ask questions.

4. Know that children have different coping mechanisms. Be aware of them.

Ch 10: Developmental Trauma: The Hidden Epidemic

Summary

Many genes work together to produce an outcome. Genes are not fixed, and life events can modify the genes' behavior. However, methylation patterns can be passed on to one's children.

Traumatized children share three characteristics: a persistent dysregulation pattern, attention and concentration problems, and attunement difficulty with self and others.

Personality, IQ, and temperament are not predictors of the child's behavioral problems during adolescence, but the parents' interaction with the child is. Consistent caregiving raised balanced individuals, while erratic caregiving yielded children who were constantly physiologically aroused. Unpredictable parents are more likely to raise attention-seeking children who are always anxious and get frustrated with even minor challenges.

Sexually abused girls take on a different developmental path. They are unable to trust, so they cannot form friendships with either gender. They tend to either overreact to a situation or simply zone out, so other children see them as weird. These girls mature sexually faster than other girls.

One Monday morning, a clinician at the Trauma Center reported that Ayesha, one of their patients, had been raped again over the weekend. She ran away from her group home, went to a druggies ' hangout in Boston, did drugs, and left with a group of boys in a car. The boys gang-raped Ayesha.

Ayesha could not articulate her needs and wants and did not know how to protect herself.

The need to address the ills that traumatized children bring to our society is real. Social support is no longer an option but a necessity, and this reality should be the pillar of trauma prevention and treatment. The damaging effects of trauma on child development should not be blamed on parents because they also need help caring for their children.

Lessons

1. Traumatized children exhibit the following common characteristics: dysregulation, attention and concentration problems, and attunement difficulty.

2. The quality of a parent's interaction with a child determines the child's behavior later in life.

3. Child abuse is a severe social problem. Social support is needed to counter the ill-effects of child abuse.

4. Sexually abused girls take on a delicate development path because they have difficulty trusting either gender.

Issues surrounding the subject matter

1. What problems does child trauma bring to our society?

Goals

1. How can you help prevent the problem of childhood trauma?

Action Steps

1. Enumerate the activities you are prepared to undertake to ease the problem of child abuse.

2. Explain briefly how each activity can achieve the goal.

Checklist

1. There is a wide array of options for preventing or managing the effects of childhood trauma, including, but not limited to the following:

    a. Volunteer to work with other parents in your community or your child's school. Hold after-school activities to hold parent education classes and to learn more about child abuse and its indicators.

b. Education children on their rights.

c. Support child abuse prevention programs to continuously hold family counseling

d. Report abuse.

2. Consider also how you discipline children and how you speak with them. Evaluate if there is something you need to change with your current style.

PART FOUR: THE IMPRINT OF TRAUMA

Ch 11: Uncovering Secrets: The Problem of Traumatic Memory

Summary

Our memory is changeable; our recollection of events and the stories we tell about it are constantly revised and updated. Our memories' accuracy depends on the intensity of emotion we felt and how meaningful the event was.

We remember insults, injuries, and pains better than pleasant news because the adrenaline released at the sign of a threat etch those incidents in our minds.

Trauma, particularly that which is derived from childhood and sexual abuse, is at the root of hysteria. There are two types of memories.

Ordinary memory is social and involves telling a story for a purpose. The traumatic memory is a reenactment of experiences that are alienating and humiliating. It is always lonely and unchanging.

People with trauma cannot put the toxic memories behind them, and yet, they seem to be incapable of assimilating new experiences. Traumatized people dissociate, creating a dual memory system.

Irene's mother was sick due to tuberculosis. Irene took care of her mother while working for a living to support her alcoholic father and paying for her mother's medical expenses. Then her mother died. Weary from stress and lack of sleep, Irene tried to revive the corpse for several hours and even tried to force medicine down her mother's throat.

Meanwhile, her father had passed out. Her aunt arrived and prepared for her mother's burial, but Irene was in denial. She had to be persuaded to attend the funeral and laughed throughout the service.

After a few weeks, she was admitted to a hospital where she was treated for amnesia for her mother's death. Occasionally, she would go on a trance-like state and stare at an empty bed, oblivious to her surroundings. She began to reenact her activities while caring for her mother.

Traumatic memories cannot be recalled at one's discretion but will surface when they are not in a normal mental state. Specific cues cause these; in Irene's case, it was an empty bed.

A lack of verbal memory characterizes trauma; people who cannot tell the story tend to act out the incident to remember repeatedly.

Lessons

1. We may be retelling the same story, but the story is altered each time it is told.

2. We have a better recall of terrible news and insults than good news and pleasantries because our adrenaline level is high when we feel threatened.

3. People in trauma have difficulty telling the story because they cannot tell a cohesive story. They tend to reenact the incident.

Issues surrounding the subject matter

1. What problems accompany dissociation?

Goals

1. How can you address dissociation?

Action Steps

1. Get enough sleep.

2. Exercise daily.

3. Set up your house and office such that all sensory items that ground you are within reach. These items may include essential oils to spray on your pillow before

sleeping to help you relax, lemon drops or hard sour candies to activate your sense of taste, a soft pillow or blanket to heighten your sense of touch.

4. Keep at least three people you love to talk to on speed dial so you can easily reach them when you sense a trigger.

5. Maintain a journal to identify your triggers.

Checklist

1. Build the first two action steps into your daily routine. Find the right time and duration for the daily exercise and make it a habit.

2. Consider other options like adopting a pet, cultivating a hobby as coloring books, painting, or playing any relaxing computer games, e.g., jigsaw puzzles.

Ch 12: The Unbearable Heaviness of Remembering

Summary

Traumatized people are prone to suffer from memory loss, especially those who suffer from childhood sexual abuse. However, the trauma can re-emerge even years later but may not be as accurate.

People recall positive experiences in an organized way: a beginning, a middle, and an end. They never forget the event but may miss out on some details. Traumatic memories, on the other hand, are disorganized. People who have them may recall some of the details clearly, but not the sequence of events.

Remembering the trauma and talking about it does not guarantee a resolution. A trauma victim may tell a vivid, coherent story of their experience, but unspeakable images and uncomfortable physical sensations may continue to unsettle them.

Trauma is devastating, unbelievable, and agonizing; nobody wants to remember it.

Nancy had her laparoscopic tubal ligation after giving birth to her third child. It should have been a routine outpatient surgery, but she was not given the suitable anesthesia amount. She became conscious after the operation began, but she could not alert the medical team because she had been given a standard muscle relaxant.

At first, Nancy could not make sense of what happened to her. She got home in a daze but went about doing her household chores. Nancy could not sleep and felt disconnected. She had difficulty concentrating on her tasks and conversations and refused to use anything that would warm up.

Four nights after the surgery, Nancy recalled what happened inside the operating room. She had flashbacks. Nancy feared going to sleep and was terrified at the sight of the color blue. She lost a lot of weight within three weeks. She found herself unintentionally lashing out at her husband.

When she went back to work at the hospital, she saw someone in a surgical scrub suit in the elevator. She had irrational thoughts, which she fought off, but that episode gave way to more flashbacks, dissociation, and fear. She avoided the elevator, the cafeteria, and the surgical floors.

Slowly, Nancy was able to piece together what happened in the operating room. She remembered waking up to the medical team's laughter as they gossiped about one of the nurses, then felt the scalpel and the warm blood flowing over her skin. Later, Nancy felt the searing pain as the surgery progressed. While she was struggling with the pain, Nancy heard the team laugh. She felt like she was being tortured. She must have moved because the nurse anesthetist warned the anesthesiologist that she was "light." The anesthesiologist then ordered the nurse to get more meds but not to put them in the chart. That was the last of Nancy's recollection.

Nancy recovered from the trauma when she had to undergo a more extensive operation in Boston. She asked for a preoperative meeting with the surgeons and the anesthesiologist to discuss her horrible experience. This time she awoke to a safe environment.

Lessons

1. Traumatic memories come out as fragmented information.

2. Traumatized people tend to suffer from memory loss, and when they do recall it, the details may no longer be accurate.

3. Articulating a traumatic experience does not necessarily mean a resolution or recovery.

Issues surrounding the subject matter

1. What difficulties can be potentially experienced by a trauma victim if they have an inaccurate account of their experience?

Goals

1. How can you address, if not prevent, "false memories"?

Action Steps

1. Revisit places that might trigger a recollection of your traumatic experience

2. Write freely and randomly – do not think about what you are writing. You need not be conscious of spelling and grammar.

3. Try reading self-help books on how to restore accurate memories.

4. Seek professional help.

Checklist

1. Assess the pros and cons of seeking an online therapist vs. that of an in-person therapist.

2. Self-help books are helpful but pick only those parts which apply to you.

PART FOUR:
THE IMPRINT OF TRAUMA

Ch 13: Healing from Trauma: Owning Yourself

Summary

Nobody can "treat" or undo a traumatic experience, but you can address its impressions on the body, mind, and soul. Trauma strips you of the feeling of being in control of yourself, and you can recover to reestablish ownership of yourself: to freely feel and know what you feel and know without shame, anger, or discomfort. You can achieve this state of recovery when you:

- Become calm and resolute
- Maintain the calm despite the reminders from your past
- Live fully in the present and be engaged with the people around you
- Be open and honest with yourself; talk about your survival mechanisms

The rational brain helps you understand your feelings' source, but it cannot eliminate emotions, thoughts, or sensations. It will enlighten you on why you feel the way you do, but it cannot change how you feel. Unfortunately, the more stressed we are, the more dominant our emotional brain becomes.

Resolving traumatic stress requires restoring the equilibrium between the rational and emotional brain. Without this balance, a trauma victim cannot function optimally. They can become disorganized and oversensitive, and prone to panic. They may manage to be somewhat in control but can quickly become depressed, rigid, and stubborn.

Traumatized people need to do a "limbic system therapy" to change post-traumatic reactions, which means being aware of our inner experience and befriending our inner self. How do we do that?

Deal with Hyperarousal.

Do yoga exercises and relaxation activities like tai-chi, tae kwon do, and capoeira.

Be mindful.

Pay attention to your sensations, label them and notice how they respond each time you shift your breathing, thinking, and posture. Observe how your body reacts to your thoughts.

Nurture relationships.

A good support network is a powerful safeguard against trauma. People in your support network can offer physical and emotional security and help you process your experience. Find someone who you can trust to join you in your recovery journey.

Seek a professional therapist, if needed. In choosing a therapist, ask about their training. Choose the one you feel comfortable with.

Express yourself in communal rhythms and synchrony.

Dancing, singing, or playing with a group allows you to connect with others. That connection can help heal you.

Learn the power of touch.

A gentle touch or hug can calm you down and make you feel safe. Relax with a therapeutic massage.

Get into action.

Put your stress hormones to good use. Go into somatic therapy and experience what it would have felt like to fight back in a situation similar to your experience.

When people remember every day or pleasant experiences, they are not re-living them. Not so for people with trauma. Telling the story helps in processing trauma, but critical brain systems must be online: it tells the victim that the incident was past and can form fragments of the experience into a coherent story.

Cognitive-behavioral therapy (CBT) repeatedly exposes a trauma patient to the stimulus but in a safe environment until they become less upset and more comfortable to talk about it. However, this treatment has not been as effective with trauma patients, especially those with childhood abuse.

Desensitization and medication are two other approaches used to treat trauma. However, these will only deaden the pain, and the relief is temporary.

Full recovery from trauma can only happen when memories of the traumatic experience are integrated into your life. When these memories no longer dominate you, you can begin to enjoy a meaningful life.

Lessons

1. We cannot undo a traumatic experience, but we can condition our mind, body, and spirit to soften the blow on our being.

2. The rational brain clarifies our feelings, but it cannot change how we feel.

3. Cognitive-behavioral therapy subjects a trauma patient to the same stimulus as the traumatic experience, but it is done in a safe environment.

4. There should be a balance between the rational brain and the emotional brain.

5. A limbic system therapy is needed to lessen the intensity of post-traumatic reactions.

Issues surrounding the subject matter

1. What do you think will happen if there is an imbalance between the rational and emotional brain?

2. What are the disadvantages of skipping a limbic system therapy?

Goals

1. What can you do to soften the impact of trauma in your life?

Action Steps

1. Select three items listed under limbic system therapy. Write them down in your journal.

2. Specify how you will accomplish each item. List down the steps you will take.

3. Identify the resources you will need to complete each item.

4. Each week, record your progress and note each item's effect on your body, mind, and spirit.

Checklist

1. Refer to limbic system therapy list of actions.
2. Make your progress monitoring consistent. Prepare a calendar if needed.

Ch 14: Language: Miracle and Tyranny

Summary

Therapists believe in the power of talk to address trauma, but it is nearly impossible to fully describe or put into words a traumatic experience. However, keeping silent about it makes a victim feel more isolated.

Hiding one's feelings saps their energy and deprives one of the opportunity to pursue worthwhile goals. It can also lead to physical illnesses and shameful, irrational behaviors. When a trauma victim opts to dismiss their reality, they also lose their sense of identity and purpose.

Acknowledging and putting a label to the experience and being listened to liberates a trauma victim from the fear and anger they have locked themselves in. It puts the victim's shame, terror, and anger into perspective, and by sharing them, they establish a connection with others.

Neuroscience says we have two forms of self-awareness. One form keeps track of ourselves across time, referring to our autobiographical self. This form organizes our experiences into a coherent narrative, which changes every time it is told, as we change our perspective, or as we add new input. The story is for public consumption and something we can accept as the truth when we repeatedly tell it.

The other form reveals the self in the present moment or moment-to-moment awareness. It is based on physical sensations but can be put into words if we feel safe. This reaction tells us how our inner self feels about the experience; we need both forms to work side-by-side to recover from trauma.

Writing is an effective way of accessing our inner self because it saves us from being judged. Since it is non-threatening, we can be candid and honest in what we write. Re-reading what we wrote also allows us to discover more truths about ourselves.

Art, dance, and music may be used as a nonverbal approach to treating trauma, but there are very little known empirical facts about how it works.

People with trauma refuse to talk about their experience, not only because it is too painful for them but also because they fear rejection of family and friends. This rejection is why trauma victims need to look for a therapist or a responsive community who can handle the truth without judgment and help them recover.

Lessons

1. A trauma victim feels more isolated if they are not able to talk about it. However, they also have difficulty putting the experience into words.

2. When a trauma victim decides to hide their feelings or ignore their reality, they lose their sense of identity.

3. There are two forms of self-awareness. One is the autobiographical self, which is for public consumption, and the other is the moment-to-moment awareness, which focuses on our inner self. We need both to recover from trauma.

4. Trauma victims refuse to recount their experiences because of shame and fear of rejection.

Issues surrounding the subject matter

1. What other potential problems can a trauma victim encounter if they do not talk about the experience?

2. What are the challenges of tuning into our inner self?

Goals

1. How can you express your feelings about your traumatic experience?

Action Steps

1. Think of nonverbal forms of self-expression and select one or two which resonate with you. Some suggestions:

   a. Write yourself a letter. Each time you recall the incident or its fragment, relate what you recall through a letter. Include your feelings and your thoughts as you recall the incident. Mention also how you felt about writing it. Always end your letter to yourself. Indicate the date when you wrote the letter so you can monitor shifts in your emotions.

   b. Poetry. It need not be measured, rhyming poetry. Write it the way you want to.

   c. Sketch, Paint, or Color. You can draw and paint on a fresh canvas, or you can use a coloring book.

   d. Art, Music, and Dance

   e. Gym Workout

   f. Martial Arts

2. Set aside a time for it. You may want to start with once weekly, and if you think it works for you, you might want to increase either the frequency or duration.

3. Document how the activity is affecting you.

4. If you think it is not for you, replace it with something else.

Checklist

1. Check out organizations near your place. They might help you source your materials or probably attend lessons if you are interested in one.

Ch 15: Letting Go of the Past: EMDR

Summary

David is a middle-aged contractor who had violent rage attacks. At age 23, while working as a lifeguard at the pool, he told a group of young men that beer was not allowed at the pool area. One of the men took out his left eye with a broken beer bottle. It has been thirty years, but the nightmares and the flashbacks won't end. His relationship with his wife and son suffered because of his trauma.

David went through a trauma recovery approach called eye movement desensitization and reprocessing (EMDR). Within seconds of the process, David was vividly recounting the entire experience. He recalled other experiences which took place before the eye-stabbing incident. He had five sessions of EMDR, and on his last session, he reported sleeping better and finding a sense of inner peace.

EMDR lets the patient focus on the internal experience without verbalizing what goes on in their inner self. What does it do?

- It helps patients see the traumatic experience from a broader context or perspective, as the patient gets access to loosely associated images and memories from their past.

- Patients get to privately observe their experience in a new way without sharing it with another person.

- Patients see their inner self even if there is no trusting relationship with the therapist.

EMDR is a process of integration and reinterpretation of memories. The resulting experience is integrated with other life events, restoring the patients' sense of agency and commitment to own their mind and body.

Research had shown that dream sleep helps in mood regulation. The lack of rapid eye movement (REM) sleep, the phase of sleep where dreaming happens, can lead to depression. Dreams link unrelated memories, and this form of creativity is also crucial to healing.

Eye movement and memory processing are typical to EMDR and REM sleep, leading some to believe they are related.

Lessons

1. EMDR is a non-threatening approach to trauma recovery that integrates even unrelated memories.

2. EMDR and REM sleep have standard features that achieve the same purpose.

3. EMDR should be administered by a trained professional.

Issues surrounding the subject matter

1. What risks accompany EMDR?

Goals

1. Learn everything there is to know about EMDR.

2. Choose an EMDR therapist you trust or feel comfortable with.

3. Discuss your concerns with the EMDR therapist. Ask questions.

4. Follow the treatment program discussed by the EMDR therapist.

Action Steps

1. Kickstart the search by just getting started. Only you will know if the therapy is for you with your own experiential knowledge.

Checklist

1. Obtain a list of certified EMDR therapists near you.

2. If time permits, see three or four therapists and discuss the treatment before selecting the therapist with who you can be at ease.

Ch 16: Learning to Inhabit Your Body: Yoga

Summary

People who are always angry or anxious usually suffer from back pain, migraine, and other chronic pain forms. They may be diagnosed and given medication for it, but they get temporary relief because the underlying issues are not addressed.

Modern neuroscience reminds us that an essential connection with our bodies secures our sense of "self." Unless we are attuned to our physical sensations, we cannot know our real selves and safely navigate life.

When we numb ourselves from the pain, we fail to provide our bodies' needs and deprive ourselves of sensory delights such as light, music, and touch. Taking care of our bodies and enjoying simple pleasures are crucial for trauma recovery.

Yoga focuses your attention on your breathing and moment-to-moment sensations. As you notice the shifts in your sensations, you take a step towards emotional control and treat your body with curiosity instead of fear.

Trauma gets you stuck in the past, but yoga changes your sense of time. Yoga strengthens you to deal with physical and emotional distress while allowing you to anticipate the end of the distress.

Lessons

1. We must be attuned to our bodies to gain a sense of self.

2. Yoga concentrates on your breathing and physical sensations.

3. We deprive ourselves of simple joys needed for trauma recovery.

Issues surrounding the subject matter

1. What are the disadvantages of yoga?

Goals

1. What can you do to counter the disadvantages of yoga and maximize its benefits?

Action Steps

1. Listen to your body and acknowledge its limits. Do not force your body to do poses it cannot handle.

2. Consult a doctor before taking up yoga.

3. Decide if you want to join a yoga class or do it on your own. If you want to join a yoga class, it might help to have a friend or relative join you in the same class.

4. Hydrate.

Checklist

1. Learn more about yoga before getting into it.

2. Access free workout tutorials on YouTube to test if your body can handle it.

Ch 17: Putting the Pieces Together: Self-Leadership

Summary

Humiliation leads us into self-preservation; we get angry, plan to retaliate or repress our feelings.

Many psychiatric problems started as adaptive strategies for self-protection. Examples of this would include panic attacks, obsessive-compulsive disorder, etc. Sometimes, the strategies take the form of learned behaviors such as aggression, depression, arrogance, or passivity. They are not diseases or permanent disabilities. Traumatic memories and adaptations will continue to haunt trauma victims until they feel safe.

Trauma victims are resilient, and how they cope is inspiring. Most children choose to self-hate than risk losing their parents or caregivers. They see themselves as unlovable so that as they grow older, you sense their lack of self-work. Adults fall into the same trap in their effort to preserve their sense of dignity.

We all have parts – our feelings and distinct ways that represent one element of our identity. Our ability to get along with ourselves depends on how attuned we are to our different parts or internal leadership skills.

The internal family systems (IFS) therapy suggests that each of us has a family-like mind where members have different levels of maturity, wisdom, and pain. A change in one part will affect all other parts. Trauma makes certain parts of ourselves carry the burden of the pain, and these parts remain locked inside. We call these parts the exiles.

Other parts unite to keep the internal family safe from the exiles. However, in keeping the harmful parts away, the protectors somehow absorb some of the energy of the abuser. Managers make sure we do not get close to anyone or push us to be productive. There are also firefighters, or emergency responders, who act spontaneously when an experience triggers an exiled emotion.

A nation or an organization can only effectively run if they have competent leadership; so does the internal family. Mindful leadership is the basis for healing from trauma. All parts of our "self" must be attended to, with the internal leader crafting a vision for the internal family and distributing available resources wisely. Mindfulness allows us to view situations with compassion and curiosity and direct us to self-care.

Exiles hold everything associated with the trauma and come in devastating physical sensations or extreme numbing. Exiles upset the levelheadedness of managers and the boldness of the firefighters. They hold the most sensitive, innocent, loving, and creative parts of the victim; locking up the exiles will inflict more pain.

Revisiting the exile and letting it go is a long process, referred to as unburdening. But the results are remarkable.

Lessons

1. Trauma victims employed adaptive strategies for their self-protection. However, these have been diagnosed as psychiatric problems.

2. Children adopt coping strategies that leave them feeling unloved. Similarly, adults choose to ignore their pain to have a semblance of self-dignity.

3. Each of us has parts that represent various elements of our identity.

4. The internal family system (IFS) therapy suggests that the parts within our self that represent different maturity levels. These parts work together as a family.

5. Our inner self has firefighters who protect us, managers who criticize and monitor us, and exiles, representing our intense emotions, thoughts, and physical sensations that we keep hidden.

Issues surrounding the subject matter

1. What is alarming about victims of child abuse using self-loath as a coping strategy?

2. What conflicts can happen between our inner self's protectors and exile? Manager and exile?

Goals

1. What can you do to prevent or correct self-hate?

Action Steps

1. Eat balanced meals.

2. Exercise regularly.

3. Keep a personal mantra to tell yourself every morning upon waking up to motivate throughout the day.

4. Choose to be with people who appreciate you for who you are.

5. Participate in community activities that increase your self-esteem.

Checklist

1. Check your local community for regular activities and find one you feel connected with, e.g., volunteer work.

Ch 18: Filling in the Holes: Creating Structures

Summary

Feelings of being unloved, ignored, or suppressed create an inner void in our self, challenging to fill in. The void makes you lose your sense of agency and self-worth. People who never felt loved or safe with anyone while growing up cannot activate the feeling of being cared for, rendering psychotherapy a futile exercise.

Restructuring your inner map is a good substitute for talk therapy. In this approach, you assign and position placeholders to represent the essential people in your life to project your inner world into a three-dimensional environment. Creating the tableau or structure effectively surfaces unexpected emotions, memories, and thoughts. You may change the tableau and observe the change's effect on you.

The approach allows you to revisit your past and revise it in a safe and supportive environment. The effect is so powerful that it creates alternative memories that meet your needs.

A part of the tableau is a non-judgmental "witness figure" who validates and reflects the protagonist's emotional state. The role-players' scripts are taken from the dialogue and direction given by the protagonist and the witness.

Structures support a trance-like state which is essential for significant therapeutic change. In this state, multiple realities exist side by side: you view the scene as an adult while bringing out your emotions when you were a child and confront your abuser while you are aware that you are talking to a different person.

Structures employ the imagination's amazing power to change the concealed, feared, and forbidden parts of your inner narratives into a visible, concrete reality.

We cannot undo the past, but creating structures offer participants a new experience – one that shows them that a better world awaits them.

Lessons

1. People who never felt loved, wanted, or cared for are strangers to those emotions. Since they do not know what these emotions feel like, they cannot give the same emotions.

2. Creating structures is an effective, safe, and exciting way of connecting one's reality to one ideal space.

3. Although there is nothing we can do about the past, the exercise gives the protagonist a feel of freely expressing their needs and feelings.

Issues surrounding the subject matter

1. What are the risks in using the structures approach?

Goals

1. How do you avoid the risks involved in the structures approach?

Action Steps

1. Map out the steps in the structures technique. When possible, make the map sequential. It is alright if the steps are written in broad strokes. It does not matter whether you use a mind map or a simple linear map.

2. For each step, identify who is involved: the witness, the protagonist, the role-players.

3. Ask: What could go wrong in each step? Write them down.

4. For each potential problem you listed, identify a preventive measure and a recovery action.

Checklist

1. You may not be a part of a trauma group that performs this exercise, but it would be interesting to evaluate how safe the technique is.

2. If you know a therapist who is into this practice or is a part of a similar group, show the therapist or witness your output to discuss your analysis's merits.

Ch 19: Rewiring the Brain: Neurofeedback

Summary

Neurofeedback is mirroring the brain's functions. An analogy would be like having a conversation with a client, and you are watching their face. Your client smiles and sends affirmation signals, so you continue making your point. However, if you see your client looking bored, frowning, or shifting their gaze, you either change the topic or wrap it up.

It is the ability to track the brain's circuitry. Our brain waves change as subtle changes in our mental state and physical sensations take place.

Neurofeedback can help change habitual brain patterns created by trauma. The change will make the brain less vulnerable to stress reactions and focus on ordinary events. It also improves our brain's resiliency, enabling us to develop more options to respond to situations. It helps reverse and prevent learning disabilities.

It is primarily helpful in addressing the confusion, hyperarousal, and concentration problems of people suffering from developmental trauma. But it can also reduce anxiety and panic attacks, address tension headaches, improve cognitive ability after a brain injury, and treat autism, among others.

Athletic control, creativity, and inner awareness are among the things that neurofeedback can improve. Neurofeedback enhances attention, concentration, and focus. Studies have been made to assess if it can help patients with attention-deficit /hyperactivity disorder (ADHD). Based on available studies, its effectiveness on ADHD is similar to that of conventional drugs.

Alpha-theta training, a neurofeedback procedure, allows us to re-experience our trauma and foster new associations.

Questions on treatment protocols for neurofeedback are still looking for answers, but so far, it has shown great potential as an intervention for trauma.

Lessons

1. Neurofeedback is about sending and receiving signals within the brain, and making sense of those signals.

2. An increase in resiliency is among the benefits neurofeedback offers. Trauma victims, by themselves, are already resilient. If we increase it further, they will cope with trauma and its effects much better.

3. Neurofeedback has a broad range of use spans from something as familiar as tension headache to something critical as post-brain injury cognitive ability.

Issues surrounding the subject matter

1. What reasons could a trauma victim have for refusing to undergo neurofeedback?

Goals

1. How can you convince a trauma victim to undergo neurofeedback?

Action Steps

1. Perform a thorough research on neurofeedback – what it is, how it's done, its advantages and disadvantages.

2. Summarize research materials into a single reference written in simple language.

3. Include testimonies of people who have undergone neurofeedback.

Checklist

1. You might want your summary checked by a professional to ensure its accuracy.

2. When possible, choose testimonials of people with a similar case as the trauma victim.

Ch 20: Finding Your Voice: Communal Rhythms and Theater

Summary

Our relationship with our bodies and their rhythms determines our sense of agency. Acting is one technique of developing that relationship.

Although research on the effects of collective activities on our mind and brain is scarce, some programs use theater to alleviate trauma's ill effects. These programs are founded on communal action to confront life's painful realities and symbolic transformation.

These theater programs are intended for emotionally and psychologically wounded people. Each program encourages these people to establish a relationship with themselves and their bodies. Participants are engaged bit by bit until they realize they are in safe company.

In the Trauma Center's Trauma Drama Program, mirroring exercises help participants connect and relax. The exercise distracts from their preoccupation with what others think about them. Theater offers a different way of accessing a full range of emotions and explore options for engaging with life.

Urban Improv develops scripted skits depicting various problems faced by students. At appropriate points, the director would freeze the action and replace one of the actors with another class member. The new actor shows how they would react to the situation. The approach lets the students see the situation as an outsider and discover different ways of reacting to it. The skit is followed by an exciting discussion of the scene, using guided questions that link the scene to their personal experiences.

The Possibility Project has actors meeting three hours weekly for nine months, writing their musicals, and presenting them to hundreds of people. Recent graduates join the production team to serve as role models for the current participants. In 2010, a program was created specifically for foster care youth. The program teaches the youth the value of interdependence.

Phase one of the program is all about team building, clarifying roles, and setting norms. The second phase involves sharing life stories, and it requires listening, learning from shared experiences, breaking through the loneliness and isolation.

Sentenced to Shakespeare focuses on each actor understanding and internalizing their lines until the words resonate with the actors.

There may not be a conclusive study on how theater can heal trauma, but it can help trauma victims get attuned to their bodies, learn from others' experiences, and regain their self-worth.

Lessons

1. Theater allows trauma victims to experience a whole array of emotions in a safe environment.

2. Trauma victims connect with themselves and with others when they join the theater. Besides developing a productive relationship with others, they also develop their self-confidence before developing their skills and facing their audience.

3. Trauma victims get to see different toxic situations, some of which are similar to their experience, as an outsider. They can observe different ways of dealing with the same situation.

Issues surrounding the subject matter

1. For a trauma victim, what are the risks of joining a theater?

Goals

1. How can you minimize the risk of theater for a trauma victim?

Action Steps

1. Set house rules for all participants that must be observed before, during, and after the skits. For

example, a participant who feels triggered by the skit may choose to leave the room for that specific skit.

2. Hold post-debriefing sessions immediately after each skit as a venue for the participants to share their feelings and thoughts.

3. Include fun games and teambuilding activities to lighten the atmosphere in the room.

Checklist

1. Seek the help of a professional therapist to assist in developing and facilitation of skits and the post-debriefs.

2. Research, work with and learn from existing drama therapy groups.

Epilogue: Choices to be Made

PTSD is not just for returning soldiers, terrorist attack victims, or disaster and accident survivors only. It is a public health issue, yet it is not given attention as much as ailments like cancer and leukemia.

Our brains are programmed to engage socially through work and playgroups. However, trauma disrupts that program as it robs people of the chance to function productively and nurture healthy relationships.

Although the medical profession has gained headway in its studies on trauma, so much still needs to be done to design effective interventions for addressing trauma. The discovery of drugs that provide temporary relief is not enough.

We need solutions that will make trauma victims feel safe and loved to develop a sense of purpose and engage in dynamic interactions with others. We need to prioritize the needs of traumatized children and adolescents. We must: protect them from the evils of abuse and violence, provide them avenues for creativity and learning, and help them grow into confident adults who control their lives and ready to become a productive member of society.

Emotionally intelligent people are tuned with their emotions and those of people around them. They know how to label their feelings and communicate them. Teaching them to recognize and name their physical sensations would be helpful.

Interventions need not be complicated and expensive. Group activities like trying to keep a beach ball in the air for as long as possible teach children to focus and conform while having fun. Communal activities like athletics, group dancing, choral singing, and theater compel children to collaborate and compromise.

Trauma warns us of man's cruelty to man, but it also reminds us of how resilient we can be.